The NUTTY FOOTY BOOK

by Martin Chatterton,
the voice of football.

PUFFIN BOOKS

Published by the Penguin Group
Penguin Books Ltd, 27 Wrights Lane, London W8 5TZ, England
Penguin Books USA Inc., 375 Hudson Street, New York, New York 10014, USA
Penguin Books Australia Ltd, Ringwood, Victoria, Australia
Penguin Books Canada Ltd, 10 Alcorn Avenue, Toronto, Ontario, Canada M4V 3B2
Penguin Books (NZ) Ltd, 182–190 Wairau Road, Auckland 10, New Zealand

Penguin Books Ltd, Registered Offices: Harmondsworth, Middlesex, England

Published in Puffin Books 1994
10

Printed in England by Clays Ltd, St Ives plc

To all the lads in the second eleven and
everyone else at Southport Trinity AFC

Kick Off

Hello and welcome
to the first ever **NUTTY FOOTY BOOK!**
We are coming to you direct from our expensive
designer office at the back of Neil's Mum's spare
bedroom. We worked to bring you the very **BEST**
football writers, the **TOP** artists, the **GREATEST**
stories and the **HOTTEST** news, but we couldn't
afford them, so me and my mates did it all.
Let me introduce the **NUTTY FOOTY**
team:

'POACHER' 'GOALHANGER' 'THE DRIBBLER'

'FLETCHO' 'SHINGUARD'

Editor in Chief, and owner of a rasping left foot:
Me! Martin 'Rasper' Chatterton.
Senior Executive in control of Image Production (drawing
the pictures): Me again.
Chief Designer (typing all the stuff on Alison's Dad's
typewriter): Neil 'Poacher' Dawkins.
Graphic Design (sticking all the bits of paper down):
Alison 'Shinguard' Jardine, Cath 'Fletcho' Fletcher.
Associate Executive Journalist (writing some stuff):
Ian 'The Dribbler' MacFarlane.
Chief Technical Assistant (cutting up the bits of paper):
Rob 'Goalhanger' Holloway.

Together, we are **THE VOICE OF FOOTBALL!**

We tell it like it is, even when we don't know what it's like or
what it is or where it is or who we are or what day it is,
because we are **THE VOICE OF FOOTBALL!**

We are the half-time orange, the last-gasp equalizer, the
perfect nutmeg, the bulging net, the game of two halves, the
muddy knees, the winning streak, the fourteen-yard slide
tackle and all the other great things about football in one
handy bite-sized pack! In other words, we are:
THE VOICE OF FOOTBALL!

Now read on. We've spared every expense to bring you the
NUTTIEST stories, the **WEIRDEST** facts, the **FUNNIEST**
jokes, plus **LOADS OF STUFF WE MADE UP!** We did this for
you, lovely reader, because we have a message for the world of
footy: sit back, Jack, here comes **THE VOICE OF FOOTBALL!**

Features

Plus ... Footy Greats! Spot The ..., Top Tips, Games, Free Gifts and more!

How to be a School ★ Footy Superstar ★

When you are watching Manchester United, or AC Milan, or Brazil or ANY top team, there is one thing that ALL the players have in common with you - they all wanted to be **school footy superstars!**
So, before you lace up your boots at Old Trafford, the San Siro or the Maracana, you'll have to follow our guide to **school footy superstardom!**

At the **Nutty Footy** office we don't mind school (much), but we LOVE football. If we had our way, we wouldn't do anything else at school EXCEPT play footy! Or maybe they could <u>combine lessons with football:</u>

Put a couple of books down at either end of the classroom, pick one side of Romans, one of the Ancient Brits and you've got a top of the table **History** match!

Or how about **Maths?** 'If the crowd at last week's City match was 43,989 and the refreshment stand sold 17,435 pies, how many people didn't get a pie?'

Science would be more fun as well. 'Today we are going to look at the effect of the Earth's magnetic pull by all going to Old Trafford to check that Ryan Giggs isn't drifting into outer space ...'

<u>However</u>, school being school, you know that they are going to find **thousands** of devious ways to spoil the fun of footy. The question is, do you have the potential to make it in the rough-and-tumble world of school footy and become a **SCHOOL FOOTY SUPERSTAR!**

Picture the scene:

A howling gale whips razor-sharp sleet across the ice-topped muddy wasteland. A thin, stray dog tries to shelter behind the goal posts which are bending in the storm-force winds.

Inside the changing rooms the players huddle together for warmth. A few of the smaller ones have started to cry. And that's when it happens. You hear something that freezes the blood (as if it wasn't cold enough already) and weakens the legs.

'OK everyone, a couple of laps around the pitch and then straight on with the game!'

It's Mr Swine, the P.E. teacher from HELL!

Of course, you might be the sort of player who LOVES freezing cold mud. The sort of player who can get the ball smacked into the back of his cold thigh and, instead of fainting with pain, can say, 'Gosh that certainly woke ME up.'

For most of us though, school football can sometimes be a **nightmare**. That's why we've come up with a **handy guide** to let you know how to survive it. After all, all those footy stars have struggled through!

1. Dealing with the sports teacher

Sports teachers who run school football fall into <u>two main types</u>:

(1) the keen type, who likes to be called 'the gaffer' on match days;

(2) the bored stiff 'I'd really rather be doing anything else on a Saturday morning but the headmaster's son plays for the team and no one else had a whistle' type.

You'll be able to get away with anything with the second type but the keen ones are a bit more difficult.

First, try this letter if you <u>really</u> don't want to play.
(Of course, TRUE superstars turn out in any weather!)

Premier League FC
Famous Ground
Big City

Dear *(teacher's name)*,

Can you please allow *(insert your name)*
to rest his legs in a comfy chair today
instead of playing football?

We've just signed him on a big contract
and we're scared he'll break something
and not be able to play for us against
Manchester United on Saturday.

Yours,

(Top manager's name here)

If he still makes you play, then you'll have to go to step 2.

2. Getting through the game

<u>Picking the team</u> is the first stage of any football lesson
and, unless you're brilliant (like me) or very big (like Colin
Stubbs in class three), you'll be waiting in line, hoping to be
chosen quickly.

As it's really embarrassing when the two captains start
arguing over you ('You have him.' 'No, you have him, he's
useless.'), the trick is to GET YOURSELF NOTICED by the captains!

You could:

(a) Get some really flashy boots so they'll think you're a fantastic player.

(b) Say something like: 'Can whatever side I'm on make sure they have a left-sided sweeper who is used to playing a 5-3-2 formation.' They'll think you're a tactical genius.

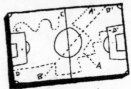

(c) Snarl, foam at the mouth or bite Neil Dawkins' knee caps. They'll think you're a psycho nutter left back.

<u>Now you're in the team</u> it's time for:

3. The game

If you're any good, there's only <u>one place</u> you want to be - <u>goal hanging</u>. In school football, most of the time the captains put THEIR MOST USELESS PLAYER in goal. This means that no matter how pathetic your shots are, they'll go in! On a good day you can't miss. Scores of over 400 each have been known.

If you can't go up front then one place to avoid is midfield. This is where all the MAD, BAD and DANGEROUS kids enjoy playing.

If it's really cold, try to get on the opposite side to Tubby Bainbridge or some other large (but useless) player. Tell the captain you'll do a man-to-man marking job on him and simply shelter behind Tubby for the rest of the game.

4. Parents

If it's a proper school match, then you'll have another problem. Parents. If they're your own, ask Mum <u>not</u> to shout out any of the following:

'Nigel, I've put a video tape in so you won't miss Postman Pat on TV.'

'Oh Nigel, your knees are getting all dirty.'

'Give Mummy a big kiss at half-time!'

<u>Dad</u>, on the other hand, needs to be careful that he doesn't argue with Jason Kinsella's dad (the one with the Rottweiler and short hair). He should also avoid invading the pitch, arguing with the referee about offside decisions or volunteering to play if your team is a player short.

<u>By following these simple steps</u> you should be able to make sure that you too are a **SCHOOL FOOTBALL SUPERSTAR!**

<u>Remember</u>, it's only a short step from the Second Year subs' bench to smashing home the winner at Wembley!

'GOOOOOAAAAAAAAAAAAAAAA AAAAAAAALLLLLLLLLLLLLLL!'

After you've scored that vital match-winning goal with a stunning thirty-yard screamer, do you:

(a) shake hands with your team mates in a polite way?
(b) turn and trot straight back to the centre circle?
(c) begin a long, complicated dance celebration?

If you answered **a)** or **b)**, then you need the **Nutty Footy Guide to After Goal Dance Steps!**

The 'Slide'. A very simple dance which involves almost

no practice. After scoring, run anywhere on the
pitch and hurl yourself feet first along
the grass, arms stretched upwards.
WARNING! Do not attempt this
on an artificial pitch or
anywhere near the
goalposts.

The 'Groove'.

This routine can be seen whenever a young player with a floppy haircut scores. Face the crowd. Point both arms at the crowd. Carefully place your left hand on your right shoulder and your right hand on your left shoulder. Drop your bottom towards the floor and give it a wiggle. Unfold your arms and point at the crowd again before running off. WARNING! On no account attempt this if you are: bald, over the age of 21, prefer the music of Phil Collins or you are facing the opponent's fans. This is because this dance has a TURKEY FACTOR of 42!

The 'Fighter Pilot'.

Popular with players who do not normally score. Because of this they go completely batty when a goal does manage to scrape in. As you score, extend both arms straight out at right angles to the body. They should now look like 'wings'. Without stopping, turn sharply away from goal and run around your team mates, arms still outstretched IMITATING A FIGHTER PILOT! Yes, it's amazingly stupid. One small tip: Do not run <u>too</u> near your team as serious injury can result.

The 'Corner Flag Samba'.

First seen during the 1990 World Cup. On that occasion Roger Milla, the Cameroon striker, scored, sprinted to the corner flag and danced the Samba with it. This has since been copied around the world, although it doesn't have quite the same exotic flavour at a January mudbath in Cleckheaton.

The Step by Step Guide

Here's one for you to practise at home.

Step 1: Keep the left leg straight with toes pointing forward. Lift the right leg and complete a double aerial back loop.

Step 2: Lift the left leg over the right shoulder. AT THE SAME TIME, extend the right arm to full length and wave at the crowd.

to After Goal Dancing.

Step 3: Place the left hand on the right ankle, grasp firmly. Place right hand on left ankle, grasp firmly.

Step 4: Thread both feet through mouth and out of ears.

Congratulations! You have completed your first Nutty Footy After Goal Dance!

NUTTY NEWS

FUTURE FOOTY
A NUTTY NEWS EXCLUSIVE!

In an astonishing exclusive, *Nutty News* can reveal details of what football will be like in the future!

Our top eggheads developed a time machine from old bits of TV sets, glue and lots of twiddly knobs. We sent our number one reporter fifty years into the future to see how the game has changed.

SHOCK!

Referees have been replaced by androids! (So no change there.)

SHOCK!

Sliding goal posts WIDEN the net as the game goes on, making it easier to score!

SHOCK!

Each team can recreate and play two guest players from history! Our picture shows Attila the Hun and Godzilla playing a nice one two just outside the box.

SHOCK!

The pitch now has specially built 'danger areas' for added thrills! Crocodile pits, quicksand and off-side traps filled with velociraptors* make certain that every player is kept on their toes!

SHOCK!

All fans wear virtual reality suits so they can actually take part in the game!

—

Players' kit will change drastically too:

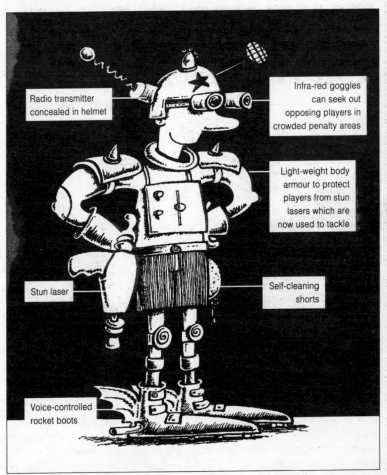

Radio transmitter concealed in helmet

Infra-red goggles can seek out opposing players in crowded penalty areas

Light-weight body armour to protect players from stun lasers which are now used to tackle

Stun laser

Self-cleaning shorts

Voice-controlled rocket boots

Phew! We can hardly wait! | *Large, vicious, meat-eating dinosaurs.*

OH NO!

It's My Mum Watching
The Cup Final!

' **I** don't really see what
all the fuss is about. After all,
it's just twenty-two overgrown schoolboys
chasing a bit of cow hide around a bit of
grass isn't it? Now which team is which? Who's
that man with the whistle? Does he kick the
ball? Why don't the players just pick the ball
up and run with it? I'm just going to put
Coronation Street on for a minute. OK! OK!
No need to bite my head off! Is there
much more of this to go? '

19

Nutty Footy Facts

Believe it or not, all these amazing facts are absolutely true!

#1

Whose side are you on? In a 1976 game between Aston Villa and Leicester City, the result was a 2-2 draw. Nothing strange about that except that Villa's Chris Nicholl scored ALL four goals!

Plymouth Argyle travelled all the way to Barrow for their November 1968 game, only to see the REFEREE score the only goal of the game! Ivan Robinson, the guilty ref, tried to leap out of the path of a shot which was going wide. The ball hit his left foot and flew into the Plymouth net.

Willie Foulkes, who played in goal for England many years ago, never worried about stopping goals. Weighing in at between TWENTY-TWO and TWENTY-SIX stone, Willie could simply sit on his line to fill the net!

Penalty shoot-outs have long been used as an exciting way to settle cup games. In June 1975 North Korea and Hong Kong drew 3-3 after extra time, forcing the game to penalties. After the teams had taken their five penalties each, the score was still level at 8-8. It was sudden death! Normally only one or two penalties are needed to settle the tie but this game needed TWENTY-EIGHT as player after player scored!

Football was originally played in the Middle Ages between teams numbering up to 500 players with goals three or four MILES apart!

Be careful if you ever find yourself in a game refereed by Kelvin Morton. In March 1989 he refereed a game between Brighton and Crystal Palace and awarded no fewer than FIVE penalties!

When Liverpool beat Crystal Palace 9-0 on 12 September 1989, EIGHT different players scored the goals! They were:
Rush,
Gillespie,
McMahon,
Beardsley,
Barnes,
Hysen,
Aldridge, and
Steve Nichol who scored two!

Not too many players can claim to have scored SIX times in one game. Denis Law did just that for Manchester City against Luton in a January 1961 cup tie, only for the referee to abandon the game after 69 minutes!

Arthur Birch scored five times for Chesterfield in the 1923-24 season. Nothing too strange about that except that Arthur was Chesterfield's GOALKEEPER! All his goals came from the penalty spot!

On the same subject, Pat Jennings, playing in goal for Tottenham against Manchester United on 12 August 1967, scored DIRECTLY from a long clearance! The unfortunate man in the other net was Alex Stepney.

Referees: A Guided Tour

Have you ever wondered exactly <u>why</u> the ref didn't give that certain penalty? Or why he was the only one who thought you were offside? Well, now you can find out as we take you on a totally biased trip around the head of that <u>man in black.</u>

1 The first thing you will notice is that there is plenty of room in there. This is because of the TINY BRAIN. Most referees do have a brain, even the one last week who disallowed that brill goal you scored, but lack of use has shrivelled it to almost nothing.

2 Next, take a close look at the eyes. See anything strange? Exactly! The connections from the eyes to the brain have been mixed up so that the ref NEVER sees that neck-high tackle on you by Dangerous Dexter McAllister and ALWAYS sees your perfectly innocent gentle push (more of a lean really) from 100 yards away in thick fog and through a crowd of players.

3 Even though his brain is so small, he has a photographic memory of every player who ever fouled, disagreed with him or didn't tuck their shirt in, so that you will STILL be in his bad books no matter when you last met.

4 Note the tiny but very sharp teeth. This means that his BITE is much worse than his bark. They also come in useful when the referee goes home for a spot of carpet chewing.

5 A rotating satellite dish on top of the ref's head is constantly monitoring, not the action in the game, but SIGNALS FROM DEEP SPACE ALIENS! Let's face it, this is the only explanation possible for most, if not all, decisions most referees make.

6 A careful look underneath the hair shows the most frightening thing. A ZIP! Yes, it's true, referees aren't human. They are ANDROIDS!

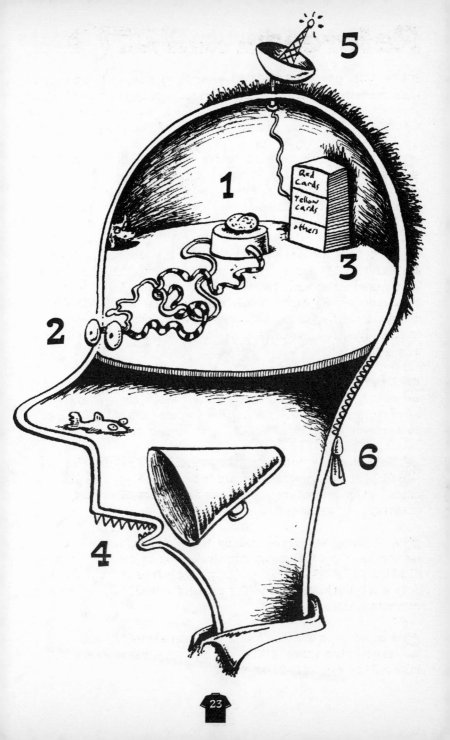

Red
Cards

Yellow
cards

others

23

No.1

Vince McVanity

Clubs: A lot

Position: Left Wing

McVanity played for 42 different teams in a six-year career. He was a magical dribbler of the ball, weaving through the opposition as if the ball was glued to his feet. Which, in fact, it was. Vince got a lifetime ban after two tubes of Superglue were found tucked into his socks.

You Are The Manager!

In this fun and easy to play game, you choose 'players' from the lists provided to come up with THE GREATEST TEAM OF ALL TIME! There are no rules. Play it with a friend and argue about which side is best.

Choose a goalie from this list:
King Henry the Eighth
Stretch Armstrong
Madonna
Daffy Duck
Norman Wisdom
Walter Zenga

Choose four defenders from this lot:
Arnold Schwarzenegger
Attila the Hun
A dalek
He-man, Master of the Universe
Fred Flintstone
A killer whale
Dennis the Menace
Tony Adams

Choose your midfield:
Brains from Thunderbirds
Albert Einstein
Sonic the Hedgehog
Genghis Khan
Billy the Kid
Beethoven
Paul Gascoigne

Strikers:
The Terminator
The monster from Aliens
Godzilla
Alan Shearer

Pick a captain for your team and decide on a tactical formation. Don't forget, this game is won by arguing!

How To Make Your Own Kit!

You know what it's like, no sooner have you spent a fortune buying your favourite team's kit than the sneaky plonkers go and bring out a new one. Add the cost of the away kit and you really need to be a millionaire to afford to support anyone these days. At the **Nutty Footy** office we've found a handy way to save money and still be the nattiest dresser on the pitch!

You will need: Paint, scissors, old newspapers, tape.

Take your old team kit and simply paint the new strip over the top. Or, if you're feeling really adventurous, design your own kit! To get that trendy multicoloured goalie shirt look, ask a few friends to throw paint at you.

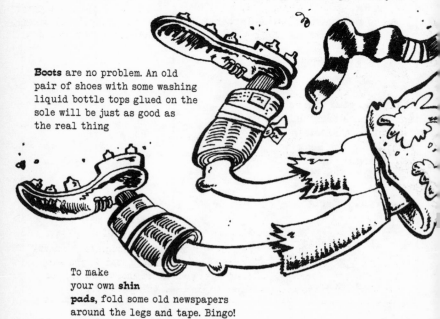

Boots are no problem. An old pair of shoes with some washing liquid bottle tops glued on the sole will be just as good as the real thing

To make your own **shin pads**, fold some old newspapers around the legs and tape. Bingo!

Here's a kit I made earlier! I think that even a professional wouldn't be able to spot the difference!

Goalie gloves can be made quite easily by tying cushions to a pair of washing up gloves. Protection and comfort!

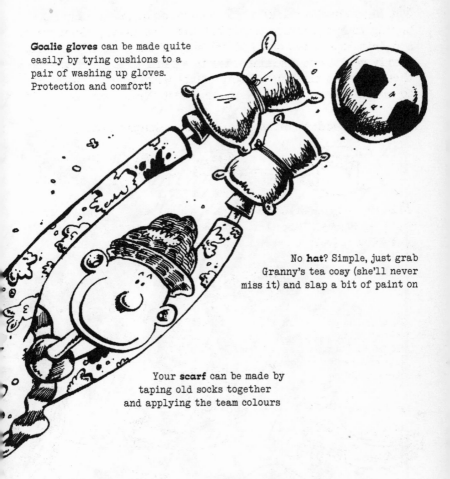

No **hat**? Simple, just grab Granny's tea cosy (she'll never miss it) and slap a bit of paint on

Your **scarf** can be made by taping old socks together and applying the team colours

Shorts are made by cutting a pair of old trousers to the right length. Make sure that they are short enough to be shorts. If you make them too long they'll be longs not shorts. If you want long shorts or short shorts, don't make your short shorts too long or your long shorts too long. Or short. Or, erm, something like that. I think.

Spot The

Ref

answer: the ref is actually in square D1

5   6   7   8

Developed at _absolutely no cost at all_ by top scientists, our
PORTASPONGE does two vital jobs in one! Concealed
under a handy _'forehead flap'_ the **_PORTASPONGE_**
cushions headers AND means you get the treatment you
need, WHEN YOU NEED IT! Simply press the flap and let
PORTASPONGE do the rest!

HAIRCUTS OF THE STARS!

Down through the years, if there's <u>one</u> thing us supporters can rely on for a good laugh, it's the never-ending parade of stupid hair styles worn by footballers the world over. Every year brings another classic to be considered for **The Nutty Hall of Shame!** Here are just a few favourites from our archives.

The 'Keegan': This shaggy, corkscrew bubble perm, named after the current Newcastle United manager, was popular during the seventies with a large number of players. The really funny thing about this cut was when it was worn long past its sell-by date. It can still occasionally be seen today on the heads of hopelessly old-fashioned players.

The 'Vinny': Designed to put total fear into the opposing team. This brutal razor crop is usually to be found on 'battling' midfield bruisers, like Vinny Jones (hence the name) and David Batty. It has been glimpsed on more artistic players, like Gianluca Vialli and John Barnes. Rumour has it that Barnes took the razor to his own locks in the dressing room shortly before a vital match against rivals Everton!

The 'Charlton': A rare sight nowadays, this style was pioneered by Manchester United's Bobby Charlton. In this cut, long side hairs are carefully combed from one side of the head to the other in an attempt to cover up an embarrassing bald spot. Of course, once the game was under way the whole thing unravelled, revealing the baldie underneath and waving around in a very silly way. The strangest thing about the 'Charlton' was that the slapheads who used it thought that NO ONE WOULD NOTICE!

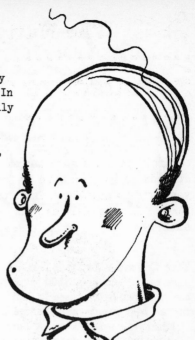

The 'I'd Really Rather Be In A Pop Group':

It's easy to spot this one as the players who wear it can be seen lounging on the wings waiting for a perfect through ball. Usually worn with a shaved and patterned back and sides.

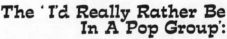

Other styles to look out for: The 'Beardsley Bowl', the 'Gullit', the 'England Manager' (grey hair, falling out in large clumps).

Great Moments in History

that didn't happen.

The Offside Trap is believed to have been discovered 3,500 years ago, but it has only been used in football for the last twenty years. Before then it had been used as a way of hunting wild buffalo. The hunting party would wait for the buffalo to get in an offside position then rush forward, shouting 'OFFSIDE REF!'. After an afternoon of this, the buffalo just gave up out of pure boredom. Much like today, really.

No Way REF!

The Free Kick is a more modern invention. Before 1898 you had to pay good money for a kick.

Half-time Tea was first brewed over two million years ago in a top of the table clash between Stonehenge Wednesday and Druids United. The original teabag is still being used today!

The Laced Football was finally replaced in 1951 after Reggie Fop, the Leyton Orient striker, TIED the ball to his boot and scored 82 times before the referee noticed!

..and for those of you watching in black and white, Everton are playing in the blue shirts...

Colour Shirts. With the invention of colour TV, all football teams had to buy new shirts. Until this point, teams had played in black and white. Colour TV did not arrive in Newcastle until much later and by then everyone was used to the kit and didn't want to change, thank you very much!

The Football Rattle Mystery. Until 1965 every single person watching a match carried one of these strange and noisy items (see diagram). Then on a damp and foggy November Saturday, they all disappeared. Our reporters have discovered that the government confiscated the lot after scientists worked out that if every team in the country scored at once, the wind produced by the 23 million rattles could tip the Earth out of the Sun's gravity field, setting the planet on a collision course with Mars. Phew! Well done chaps!

For all you budding referees out there!

Simply follow the instructions and you'll be the proud owner of those essentials in any ref's kit ... **the red and yellow cards!**

Great free Gift!

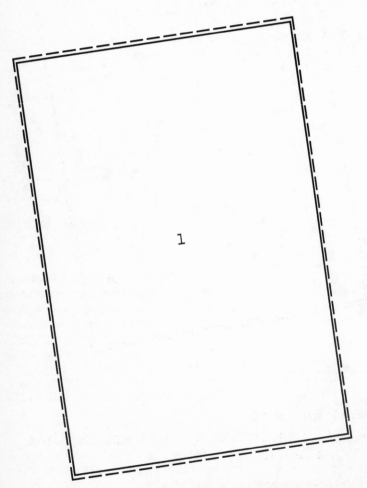

1

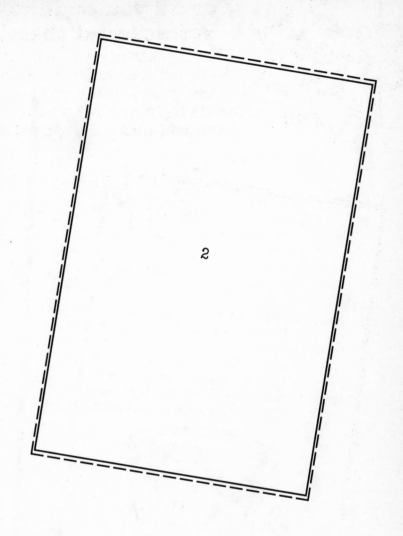

2

Instructions: ✏️ ✂️
colour in as indicated by the numbers, then
cut around the dotted line.

Key: 1 - yellow; 2 - red

Footy Food

Recipes

Football Tea

You will need:
1 pair of dirty footy socks
56 pints of dish water
1 teabag
Toenail clippings

Boil your dish water. Place the teabag in one of the socks and fill teapot as usual. Allow the 'tea' to stew for at least three days. Reheat in a microwave (for that authentic metallic taste), add a sprinkle of toenail clippings and serve. The tea should be totally undrinkable. (Handy tip: if you have any left over, Football Tea makes perfect paint stripper.)

Half-time Pie.

You will need:

Very old pastry
Water
Air
That really horrible jelly you always get in meat pies
Some old school erasers

This is a simple recipe to prepare the perfect half-time pie. Take the pastry and bash it into a round shape. Don't worry if it looks as though it has been trampled by the Stretford End, that's exactly what it should look like. Next, fill the pie with the air, water, jelly and erasers. (Note: if you can't get any erasers, fill with absolutely any old rubbish lying around.) To get the pie to the correct temperature, place it in a Thermonuclear Reactor Core. This should see to it that the pie burns the roof of your mouth as red hot jets of steam and water shoot out.

Nutty Footy Facts

Even stranger true facts from the world of footy!

#2

The fastest goal on record is timed at FIVE seconds by Malcolm Macdonald of Newcastle United. Supermac simply smacked the ball past the astonished keeper FROM THE KICK OFF!

KEEPING IT IN THE FAMILY:
Ian Bowyer played alongside his son Gary for Hereford United against Scunthorpe in 1990, the first time this had happened for 39 years. Brothers Alan and Gary Kelly were the opposing keepers when Preston played Bury on 13 January, 1990. Father Alan Snr, who had kept goal himself for Preston, was there to see it!

Bill Lambton didn't get a vote of confidence from his club chairman. He wasn't there long enough. Appointed manager of Scunthorpe United in April 1959 he lasted just THREE days in the job!

12 September 1885 is a day remembered fondly in Arbroath. In a Scottish Cup match they whupped the unlucky Bon Accord 36-0! Incredibly, Dundee beat Aberdeen 35-0 on the same day, in the same competition, making a two-match goal tally of 71!

Snooze corner. In the 1978-79 season, Norwich City drew 23 times in 42 games, the most draws ever recorded.

Jack Kelsey had to be quick off the mark after he had played for Wales in a 2-2 draw against England at Villa Park in Birmingham on 26 November 1958: he was due to play for Arsenal that evening 100 miles away at Highbury in London. He got there and Arsenal won 3-1 against Juventus.

You could be forgiven for thinking that if FOUR goalies played in the same game the result would be a scoreless draw. When this actually happened, the score was 5-2 to Everton against Manchester City! City substituted first choice goalie Martyn Margetson for Andy Dibble, while Neville Southall was replaced by Jason Kearton in Everton's goal.

On 1 February 1936 it rained goals: 209 were scored in 44 matches in the English Football League!

You would think that after going to all the trouble of winning the World Cup, teams would take good care of it. In fact, it has been stolen TWICE! The first time was in 1966 in London when it was eventually found by a dog called Pickles. In 1983 the cup was stolen for a second time in Brazil! Unfortunately, Pickles wasn't around to stop it being melted down!

In 1937 Manchester City scored more goals than anyone else in the First Division: 80. The trouble was they let in a lot more that season and were RELEGATED!

OH NO!

It's The Man With The Long Memory!

'You youngsters don't know
you're born. When I were a lad we never
had seats to watch footy! We had to stand!
And because crowds were bigger, we had to get in
early. Back in 1923 I stood in me vest for forty-two
hours in a raging blizzard to watch Hartlepool play
Huddersfield and there were 173,000 people in the
ground and another three million trying to get in and
we had no floodlights so all the crowd had to hold
candles so players could see ball and pitch were a mud
bath. It were so bad the referee used a boat. The goalies
sat on the crossbar to see and fourteen players drowned.
The game wasn't called off though. It took more than a
bit of mud to stop games in them days. Hartlepool won
56-0 'cos back then they knew how to score goals. Tommy
Plain scored all 56 goals AND he played with both
legs broken. After game I walked back home
37 miles across moor carrying our kid who'd
passed out on account of not having eaten
for three days. I had to fight
off a pack of wolv . . .'

Top Tips from the Nutty Footy School of Excellence!

Number **1** - Ball control

If you have trouble with your ball control, try using a whip and a chair to bring the round little blighters under control. Don't stand for any nonsense! Follow our instructions to achieve perfect obedience from your ball. Grasp the chair (1) firmly to fend off any sudden movements the ball might make. Holding the whip (2), crack it to scare the ball into doing exactly what you want. A few weeks' practice should see you becoming an expert at controlling your ball!

The Nutty Collection Of Footy Greats

No.2

Terry 'The Terminator' Gruffbloke

Clubs: Preston, Blackburn, Strangeways
Position: Centre Half

'Like a half-trained Rottweiler but nastier,' was how one manager described Gruffbloke after their teams had met. In that match 'The Terminator', who played in hobnailed boots and trained on a diet of chips, lard and Irn Bru, collected the 197th booking of his career, broke three players' legs (during the warm-up) and ate the referee.

Spot The

..... Foul

answer the foul is actually in square D7

Good evening and welcome to another Pitch of the Day. In tonight's programme we've got top-level grass cutting and turf trimming from all over the country, as well as mower action from the lower divisions. First, here's a glimpse of the type of excitement we've got coming up later in the programme.

He's going all the way, he's going all the way! Oh I say, you don't get much closer than that with a rotary strimmer!

That's just a taste of the excellent grass cutting which took place earlier today at Highbury. There'll also be some turf replacement from Liverpool and from Ibrox we've got highlights of Jock Shears' magnificent team putting the nets up. But first, over to John Motley who's talking to Nottingham Forest's controversial groundsman, Stan Bloke.

Stan. A good result?

Well with that rain we had earlier on in the week, I had my doubts, but the lads pulled together and got a result we deserved.

Now Stan, some people have said that Forest's ground won't be ready for the game today.

John, I've been working at Forest for twenty years now and people have told me every week that the grass is too long or the posts needed a lick of paint. You've just got to forget the pressure, put your head down and get on with it.

As you say Stan, you've been in the game for twenty years. What do you think of the recent flood of groundkeeping talent leaving this country for Italy?

It's the way of the world John. Them lads that have gone are after good money, but for me it's the challenge of getting a billiard table surface out of lumpy porridge that keeps me here.

Wise words indeed. Dickie.

51

NUTTY NEWS

MUTANT FOOTBALLERS FOUND ON MOON!

Believed to be a goalkeeper.

Top boffins reported today that recent pictures from a secret space mission show scenes that will send shock waves through the footy-loving world!

In amazing photos *Nutty News* can reveal that SUPER MUTANT FOOTBALLERS are being created in underground laboratories on the Moon! A bloke we spoke to said, 'This is the end of footy as we know it! I blame Graham Taylor and the introduction of the long ball game.'

Scientists have told *Nutty News* that the weird players are good enough to beat any team on this planet. And no wonder! Just look at the evidence.

The estimated speed of this player is 500 mph.

An alien centre forward?

Nutty Footy Facts

They're unbelievable! And They're all TRUE!

#3

The fastest booking ever recorded in a first-class game was one given to Vinny Jones of Chelsea in a game against Sheffield United on 15 February 1992. It took Jones just THREE seconds to collect his yellow card! In the previous year Jones had been booked after only FIVE seconds of a game <u>for</u> Sheffield United! Vinny is pipped for the fastest sending off by Guiseppe Lorenzo of Bologna, sent off after TEN seconds of the game against Parma, 9 December 1990.

The meanest defence title must belong to the Scottish club Queens Park. This miserly lot didn't have a single goal scored against them in their first SEVEN seasons!

Southend United missed their SEVENTH penalty in a row against Wolves on 28 September 1991, the worst-ever missed penalty sequence!

6 January 1934 was an unlucky day for goalkeeper Steve Mitton. On his debut for Halifax at Stockport, he let in THIRTEEN goals, making him the unluckiest goalie in history!

The average length of time that the ball is in play in a football match is just 52 minutes!

Mark Dennis, the QPR defender, holds the title of longest suspension - 53 days. He got this in November 1987 after collecting the ELEVENTH sending off of his career. Dennis had also been booked 64 times!

In February 1905, Alf Common became the world's most expensive transfer after Middlesbrough paid Sunderland £1,000 for him. Eighty-seven years later, the record stood at £13,000,000 when Gianluigi Lentini left Torino for AC Milan! This is a price increase of £12,999,000! At the other end of the scale, Torquay United paid Whitley Bay six FOOTBALLS for the services of Ian Johnson in November 1992!

It's a rare event for a player to score five goals in one game. Tony Woodcock did just that for Arsenal against Aston Villa on 29 October 1983. What is really peculiar about this is that Ian Rush scored five for Liverpool against Luton ON THE SAME DAY!

Cambridge United didn't have much to smile about in the 1983 season. They didn't win ANY games between 8 October and 23 April in the following year! This run of 31 games (21 lost, 10 drawn) is the worst run of footy luck in the Football League.

On the other hand, Nottingham Forest didn't lose for 42 matches between November 1977 and December 1978! They won 21 and drew 21, the longest unbeaten sequence in League history!

The Nutty Armchair

We can't afford to go to all the games we want - the World Cup, for example, or that crucial, all-ticket FA Cup semi-final. But watching the game on TV isn't quite the same. The electric atmosphere, the smells, the roar of the crowd, the stale pies. At **Nutty Footy**, however, we have spared no thought or effort to overcome this problem by developing the **Nutty Armchair Simulation** system. Simply follow our instructions and you will be able to recreate the atmosphere of a <u>live game</u> as you watch it on TV.

1. Preparing the grandstand

To get that special, really uncomfortable feeling you can only get from a stand seat, place a short plank on the armchair seat. This should quickly make your rear end go completely numb.

2. Getting the weather right

Using only a household ladder and a watering can, you will be able to simulate that refreshing, completely soaked feeling as the rain sweeps in from Siberia.

Footy Simulator

3. The Fans

Invite around all the people you really hate and get them to sit very close to you. It makes it more convincing if they have to squeeze past you every time they go to the toilet.

4. The view

If you have a nice clear view of the telly, this can be put right easily by simply placing a large person, or a sixteen-foot length of heavy duty girder, right in front of you.

5. The Food

It is very important to make sure you have the correct refreshments. You'll have to prepare your pies, tea and watery orange juice in advance. To get that horrible taste just right, use our recipes on pages 38/39.

6. The Mexican Wave

No big match is complete without a Mexican wave. You can create your own by inviting a few friends round and sitting in a row.

No.3

Barry Pounce

Clubs: Liverpool, Everton, Airdrie
Position: Centre Forward

Pounce lived up to his name throughout his goal-littered career, scoring over 500 goals with his lethal left foot. Unfortunately Pounce never got the recognition he deserved as he also scored 342 own goals. This was put down to both Pounce's colour blindness and the fact that he always forgot to change round at half-time.

You'll Never Be Nutty Alone!

GREAT FOOTBALL SONGS TO LEARN AND SING

Number 1 : 'Ere We Go'

The lyrics are quite difficult so attention is needed.

> 'Ere we go, ere we go, ere we go,
> ere we go, ere we go, ere we go-oh,
> ere we go, ere we go, ere we go,
> ere we go, ERE WE GO!'
>
> (Chorus)
> 'Ere we go, ere we go, ere we go,
> ere we go, ere we go, ere we go-oh,
> ere we go, ere we go, ere we go,
> ere we go, ERE WE GO!'

Number 2 : 'One Nil'

Again, you'll need to concentrate.

> 'One nil,
> one nil,
> one nil,
> one nil,
> one nil,
> one nil,
> one nil.'

Number 3 : 'You're Not Singing Any More'

> 'You're not singing any more,
> you're not singing any more,
> you're not singi-ng any-more!'

Remember, <u>practice makes perfect</u>, so be sure to keep belting these out at the breakfast table!

Back-Page

Simply fill in the blanks.

[   ] IN DEMOLITION DEBUT!

In a stunning first half display, [   ] yesterday destroyed Premier League, high-flying United with a ten-goal explosion.

Playing his first-ever full game for [   ] FC this young genius carved out goal after golden goal. Although only [   ] years old, [   ] blasted through what had been a rock solid defence. Showing a cool head, this young player with film-star looks, volleyed, chipped and stroked the ball all over the pitch. [   ] RACED on to a through ball past the United back four to open his account with a low piledriver from 30 yards after just TEN seconds!

Without giving the crowd a chance to settle, [   ] won the ball in his own box and galloped the length of the pitch to chip the advancing keeper for number two.

Nothing the United squad of internationals could do got in [   ]'s way. A third goal came shortly before half-time from a blistering HEADER!

Hero!

NUTTY NEWS

your face here

After the break, the floodgates opened and [   ] ran riot, scoring at will. At the final whistle, ecstatic fans carried him from the pitch.

A stunned United manager said afterwards, '[   ] was the best player I've ever seen with the possible exception of Ryan Giggs.'

[   ] FC denied rumours that a £47 million transfer bid had come from Italian giants AC Milan.

Spot The... Fan

answer: the fan is actually in square C3, next to the polar bear. In a blizzard.

Household Hints For Out of Date Footy Wear!

Don't throw away that old scarf! Hold on to those boots! Keep those mud-encrusted shorts! With just a little effort you can put those worn-out items to use by following our handy household hints!

Here are some of our ideas:

Old scarves

Keep Dad's wig secure in high winds

Cleaning your ears

Keeping fit

Make a delightful tablecloth

Elastic gone? No panic!

Horror movie watching in comfort

Emergency shoelace

Learn snake charming without the danger

Cheer up that old dog lead!

Make a delightful and unusual pot for Mum's cheeseplant!

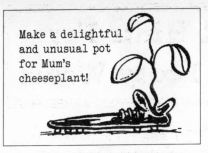

Old boots

Take out the old studs and make an attractive necklace!

Those laces can be saved and woven into fashionable underwear!

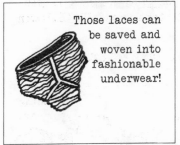

Replace that boring door knocker with an old boot dipped in bronze!

Give the hamster an exciting new home!

Collect half a dozen, sew together and hey presto! a new duvet cover!

Old shirts

Cut up into squares, boxed and embroidered they make ideal Christmas hankies!

We hope that you'll be able to have endless hours of fun and profit from your old kit! We have!

OH NO!

It's The Loony Fan
Who Never Shuts Up!

'**G**ERROFFYOU
DOZYLUMPALARD!Youareabout
asusefulasachociceattheNorthPole!
Idon'tknowwhythemanagerpickshimhe
mustknowsomethingIreckonheshouldhave
passedtoRushyorSmithythensprinted
crossfieldtogetthereturnandbeatenthem
sixdefendersandslicedorbenttheball
overthekeeperwiththeoutsideofthe
bootlikethemBrazilians
s'obviousinnit?'

The Great
Nutty Footy Quiz

(The answers are at the bottom of the page)

1 - What is the only professional club in Britain whose name begins with the letter K?

2 - How old was Paul Allen when he became the youngest player to take part in an FA Cup final?

3 - Who plays at Carrow Road?

4 - Which team is known as The Potters?

5 - What did Sam Widdowson wear for the first time in 1874?

6 - How old was Sir Stanley Matthews when he played for Stoke City on 6 February 1965, becoming the oldest player to appear in the First Division?

7 - What is the world's largest football stadium?

8 - Name the two clubs who share a stadium in Milan.

9 - What is the award given to the player who scores the most goals in Europe called?

10 - Whose nicknames are: The Toffees, The Canaries, The Blades, The Rams, The Dons, The Magpies?

11 - If a team wins the World Cup three times does it keep the trophy?

12 - Which English club plays in the Scottish League?

13 - What is the average amount of time that a ball is in play during a 90-minute game?

14 - Which English club was the first top-class side to install artificial turf?

15 - What is the largest crowd ever to watch a match in Britain?

16 - Who plays at Filbert Street?

17 - Which club's song is 'I'm Forever Blowing Bubbles'?

18 - Can you name the oldest professional club in Britain?

19 - Who played in the first ever floodlit League game?

20 - Which Welsh teams play in the English League?

21 - In what month does the Scottish League Cup Final take place?

22 - What is the home ground for the Republic of Ireland?

23 - Who knocked the Republic of Ireland out of the 1990 World Cup?

1 - Kilmarnock. 2 - 17 years and 256 days. 3 - Norwich. 4 - Stoke City.
5 - Shin pads. 6 - 50 years 5 days. 7 - The Maracana in Rio de Janeiro,
Brazil, capacity 165,000. 8 - AC and Inter Milan. 9 - The Golden Boot.
10 - Everton, Norwich City, Sheffield United, Derby County, Wimbledon,
Newcastle United. 11 - Yes. 12 - Berwick Rangers. 13 - 52 minutes. 14 - QPR.
15 - 149,547, Scotland v England, Hampden Park, 1937. 16 - Leicester City.
17 - West Ham. 18 - Notts County, 1862. 19 - Portsmouth v Newcastle, 1956.
20 - Swansea, Wrexham and Cardiff City. 21 - October.
22 - Landsdowne Road. 23 - Italy.

69

BUILD YOUR OWN
ARMOURED SHIN PADS!

Those miserable little plastic planks strapped around your legs will look *pretty pathetic* next to these <u>armour plated, fully riveted, flame proof, tempered steel</u> **TANK PADS!**

Precision cut from ex-Army tank plating and assembled <u>at home</u>, the **TANK PADS** *will have any leg biter thinking twice!*

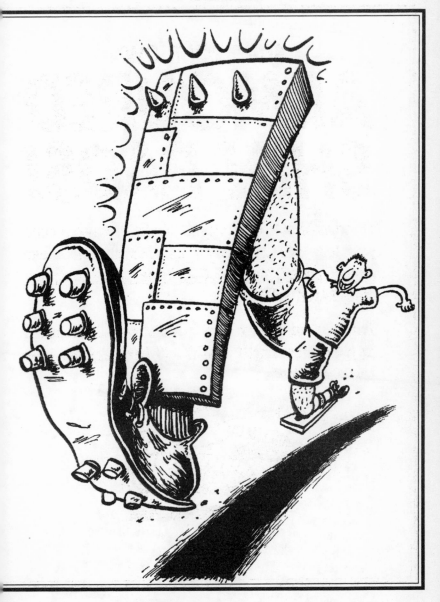

No.4

Rupert Twistleton-Squirrel Smythe
Farquharson the Third

Clubs: Chelsea

Position: Goalkeeper

One of the few professional footballers from the public schools, Farquharson played for only one club, Chelsea in London. He turned down a transfer to Manchester United on the grounds that it was too far from his tailors. Despite this he had a glittering career in goal, the only real difficulty being for the fans trying to sing 'There's only one Twistleton-Squirrel Smythe Farquharson the Third, one Twistleton-Squirrel Smythe Farquharson the Third...'

Top Tips
from the Nutty Footy School
of Excellence!

Number **2**. - Beating the Offside Trap

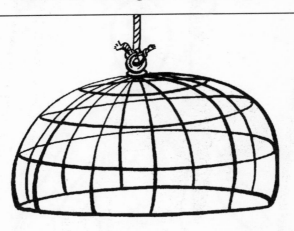

Preparation is vital if you are to master the art of beating the offside trap. The Nutty Footy method is to act like nothing interesting is happening, whistle, or read the paper. Then just as the trap is sprung, make a break for it! If you do get nabbed, get your mum to smuggle a file in baked in a cake.

⊘ **Build Your Own Player!** ⊖

Nutty Footy gives you a chance to construct your <u>very own football player.</u> Just copy the bits on to paper and paste on to the model to make the perfect player.

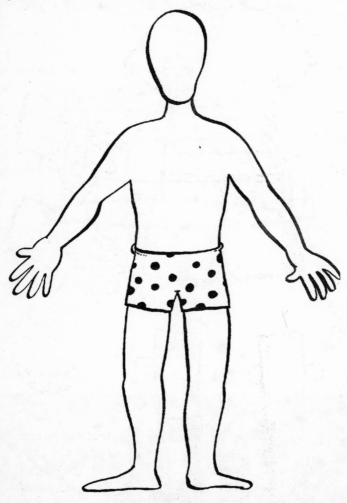

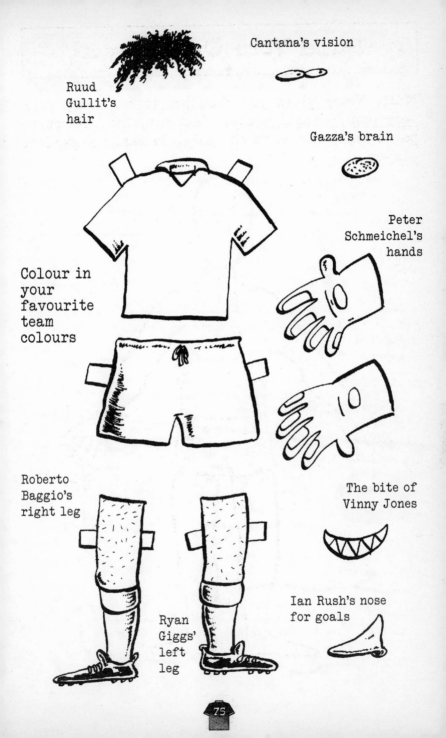

Ruud Gullit's hair

Cantana's vision

Gazza's brain

Peter Schmeichel's hands

Colour in your favourite team colours

Roberto Baggio's right leg

Ryan Giggs' left leg

The bite of Vinny Jones

Ian Rush's nose for goals

Did They Really Say That?

Footballers, managers and commentators are well known for saying some stupid things. Here are just a few of them! And don't forget ALL the quotes here are absolutely TRUE!

> 'I never predict anything and I never will do.'
> *Paul Gascoigne*

> 'It's a good job I'm not colour blind because both teams are playing in black and white.'
> *Harry Gration*

> 'He's captain of Rangers and that's one of the reasons he's captain.'
> *Walter Smith*

> 'Without picking out anyone in particular, I thought Mark Wright was tremendous.'
> *Graeme Souness*

> 'Trevor Steven might have scored there if he'd chanced his arm with his left foot.'
> *Trevor Brooking*

> 'On the night it just wasn't our day.'
> *Ron Atkinson*

> 'If we score more goals than they do, we will win.'
> *Kenny Dalglish*

'I can see the carrot at the end of the tunnel.'
Stuart Pearce

'I can count on the fingers of one hand
ten games where we've caused our own downfall.'
Joe Kinnear

'There's no job in football I've ever wanted.
This is the only job in football I've ever wanted.'
Kevin Keegan

'There are two ways of getting the ball - one way
is from your own players and that's the only way.'
Terry Venables

'Let's close our eyes and see what happens.'
Jimmy Greaves

'There's no such thing as an easier route, but it's an easier route.'
Bobby Robson

'Chris Waddle is off the field at the moment;
exactly the position he's at his most threatening.'
Gerald Sinstad

'There's one that hasn't been cancelled because of the
Arctic conditions - it's been cancelled because of a frozen pitch.'
Bob Wilson

And The Winner Is...

The Nutty Footy 'Best Footballing Actors' Awards

<u>Every year</u> a glittering audience sees the most talented movie stars in the world get their reward at the Hollywood Oscars ceremony. At the **Nutty Footy office,** however, we think that the performances of Bruce Willis and the rest of the hams are only a pale imitation of the REAL actors out there on the footy pitch.

<u>So, without further ado,</u> here are some of the nominations for Best Acting performance in recent years.

The Award for the
'**Most Acrobatic Dive**' goes to . . .

<u>JURGEN KLINSMANN</u> of Germany for perfecting the dive with double twist and back flip, otherwise known as the 'Klinsmann Roll'. The judges were particularly impressed by Jurgen's ability to show extreme pain, produce real tears and collect dozens of penalties without a defender EVER appearing to touch him!

The Award for the
'Best Team Effort' goes to …

<u>ROBERTO ROJAS</u>, the captain and goalkeeper of Chile. We really liked his performance in the 1989 World Cup qualifier against Brazil. With Chile needing a win and Brazil winning 1-0, the game looked lost. But, as one of the 160,000 spectators threw a flare towards him, Roberto suddenly clasped his hands to his head and fell dramatically to the floor, as if he had suffered a cut to the forehead. His team mates rushed to his side and carried him from the field. Brazil would surely be chucked out of the World Cup! After an investigation by FIFA, however, it was discovered that the flare had missed Rojas, the Chilean team doctor had NOT treated the goalie for cuts and an official had burnt Roberto's bloodless gloves and shirt! What a performance!

n

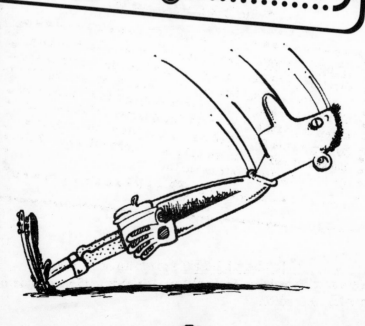

Now that's what I call the Hand of God...

The 'Who Me?' Award goes to . . .

DIEGO MARADONA of Argentina for what seemed to be a
thrilling and skilful use of the hand in punching the
ball into the England net AND GETTING AWAY WITH IT!
'It was the hand of God,' claimed Diego, in an interview
after the vital 1990 World Cup quarter final was won
by Argentina 2-1. Of course it was Diego, you complete
bucket of swi . . . (there will be a short interval while
we try to calm down the Editor).

Why not try this one at home? Think up some new
categories: **Best Dive in the Box, Pinching 15 yards at a
throw-in,** and so on!

ATTENTION ALL
GOALIES!

DO YOU EVER GET THE FEELING that the ball's been *coated in butter*?

OR that you would have more chance *catching an eel in your teeth* than *stopping a goal?*

Well, worry no more!

With our amazing **INFLATABLE GOALIE GLOVES**, *you won't need to catch a thing!* Simply *pull the rip cord* and **Hey Presto!** your gloves *instantly expand* to block the goal!

Even the deadliest strike will bounce *harmlessly away* as you look on!

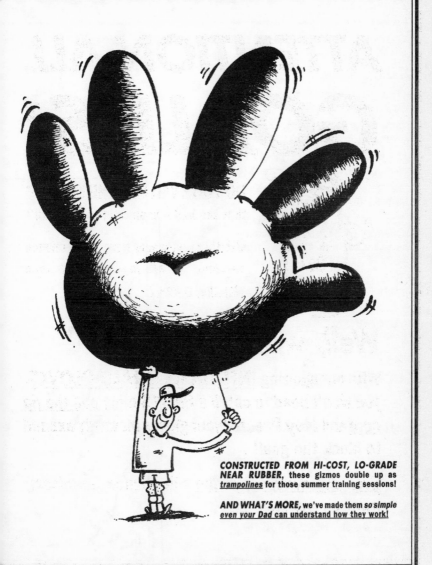

CONSTRUCTED FROM HI-COST, LO-GRADE NEAR RUBBER, these gizmos double up as _trampolines_ for those summer training sessions!

AND WHAT'S MORE, we've made them _so simple even your Dad_ can understand how they work!

83

The Nutty Footy

Can you complete the crossword?

Clues Down:

1. The cup played for at Wembley every year in May (1,1)

3. How many yards must the wall go back at a free kick? (3)

4. If you win the ball from an opponent in the playground? (5, 6)

5. Large stringy thing that stops the ball (3)

7. The ref will blow for this if there are no defenders between the attacker and the goal when the ball is played (7)

9. Second name of Manchester's Red Devils (6)

10. If he's quick, you might say he had this (5)

13. It's round and hollow (4)

Clues Across:

2. If you get sent off, you'll be taking an early one of these (4)

4. Bits of your legs protected by guards (5)

6. If you score 2 and they score 1, you have done this (3)

8. A game lasts 90 of these (7)

11. The man with the whistle (3)

12. Sits on the bench, he might come on (10)

14. Opposite end of your foot from your toe (4)

15. This team plays at Elland Road (5)

Crossword!

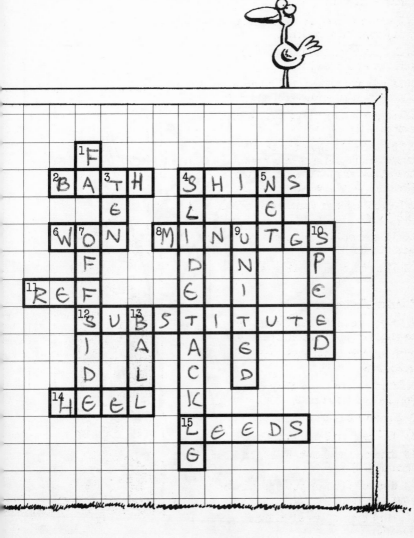

Across:

- 2. BATH
- 4. SHINS
- 6. WON
- 8. MINUTG
- 11. REF
- 12. SUBSTITUTE
- 14. HEEL
- 15. LEEDS

Down:

- 1. F
- 3. TEN
- 5. NET
- 7. OFF
- 9. UNITED
- 10. SPEED
- 12. SIDE
- 13. BLACK

Top Tips
from the Nutty Footy School
of Excellence!

Number 3. - Dribbling

The art of dribbling is actually quite easy to become expert at. Just take a big mouthful of water (fig. 1), and try to speak. You'll find dribbling no problem at all!

No.5

Osvaldo Rodriguez Fortunato

Clubs: Tottenham, Newcastle, Motherwell
Position: Midfield genius

Fortunato was one of the first foreign players in the British leagues. With an excellent football brain, he looked certain for a wonderful career until he did one of the most horrible things possible for a footballer: he released a 'comedy' record and it got to number one in the charts. The fans never really forgave him and 'Little Os' returned to Argentina a broken man.

Your Letters

Dear Ed,
I'm just writing to complain! I like to complain about anything very strongly! It doesn't matter what you've got, I'll complain about it!
Yours,
Annoyed of Basildon
P.S. Can I have a T-shirt?

Dear Ed,
Can you tell me why, at football grounds, the stands are where you sit?
Yours,
Nigel Stupid, East Grinstead

No.

Dear Ed,
My mate fancies you something rotten.
Yours,
Tracy Morrison and Michaela Smith, just behind you in Mrs Parker's class.

How did that one get in here?

Dear Ed,
I'm a mad keen Torquay United fan.
I've been ...

(Ed: this letter is being stopped on the grounds that this person obviously needs medical help immediately)

Dear Ed,
Can you settle an argument that me and my mates are having? I say that in the third round of the 1922 Bert Snug Trophy, Aggregate United playing Shovehapenny Rovers in a second replay had a man called Smith in the line-up. They say his name was Smythe. Which was it?
Yours,
Puzzled of Oswaldtwistle

Zzzzzzzzzzzzzzzzzzzzzzzzzzzzz.

Dear Ed,
The book you borrowed, 'Shin pads: An Illustrated History', is now overdue and MUST be returned forthwith.
Yours,
Southport Public Library

Final whistle

The referee is looking at his watch, there can't be too much time left, can there Des? We have had quite a few stoppages though and there may still be time to get a few more Nutty things in before this book finishes.

And here's the young international, 'Goalhanger' Holloway coming up on the left of the typewriter with what looks like a couple of promising funny bits. He's got past the chair, dummied the door and here he goes! 'How many footballers does it take to change a lightbulb?' Oh, he's gone for a difficult one, Des. Here comes the answer but will it be enough to get a laugh from this crowd? 'It takes eleven players to change a lightbulb. One to put it in and ten to give him a big kiss for doing it.' I don't think that will be enough to finish off this book, Des, but there might still just be time for another effort. 'Some flies were having a game of footy in a saucer. They won and next week they'll be playing in the cup.' No, it looks like it will take more than a few stale attempts like that one to finish this book. The referee has the whistle in his mouth (well Alison's Dad wants his typewriter back) and what's this? Some people are on the back page, they think it's all over! It is now!